The Funny Song-book

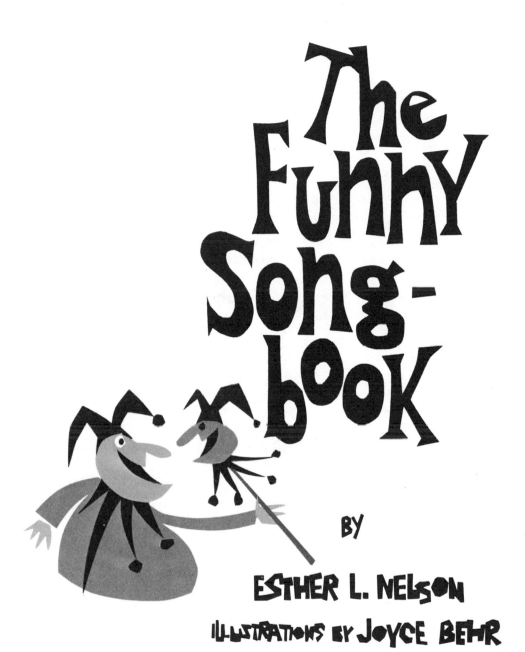

BY

ESTHER L. NELSON

ILLUSTRATIONS BY JOYCE BEHR

Sterling Publishing Co. Inc. New York

Other Books of Interest
Best Singing Games for Children of All Ages
Dancing Games for Children of All Ages
Holiday Singing and Dancing Games
Movement Games for Children of All Ages
Musical Games for Children of All Ages
Silly Songbook
Singing and Dancing Games for the Very Young

Library of Congress Cataloging in Publication Data
Main entry under title:

The funny songbook.

For voice and piano ; with chord symbols for guitar.
Summary: An illustrated collection of sixty, easy-to-play, humorous songs including camp songs, parodies, Bible songs, and silly ditties.
1. Children's songs. 2. Humorous songs. [1. Songs.
2. Humorous songs] I. Nelson, Esther L. II. Behr, Joyce, ill.
M1997.F996 1984 84-89
ISBN 0-8069-4682-2
ISBN 0-8069-7832-5 (pbk.)
ISBN 0-8069-4683-0 (lib. bdg.)

Seventh Printing, 1986

Copyright © 1984 by Esther L. Nelson
"The Swiss Cheese Song" © 1976
Sarah Pirtle, reprinted by permission.
"The Gum Song" © 1975 Mary Feeny
Dart, from *Songs for People*, reprinted by permission.
"Old Mrs. Lazibones" © 1978 by Gerda
Mayer, Music by Wynn Hunt, reprinted from *The Knockabout Show*, Chatto & Windus (London).
Published by Sterling Publishing Co., Inc.
Two Park Avenue, New York, N.Y. 10016
Distributed in Australia by Oak Tree Press Co., Ltd.
P.O. Box K514 Haymarket, Sydney 2000, N.S.W.
Distributed in the United Kingdom by Blandford Press
Link House, West Street, Poole, Dorset BH15 1LL, England
Distributed in Canada by Oak Tree Press Ltd.
% Canadian Manda Group, P.O. Box 920, Station U
Toronto, Ontario M8Z 5P9
Manufactured in the United States of America

Thanks to my friends—young, middle-aged and old—who have contributed to this collection of songs: Karen Levine, Lillian Enfield, Barbara Fisher, Susan Braiding, Sheila Gladstone, Noah Feinstein, Walter Moxon, Fay Storch, Joy Yelin, Gerry Hill, Ruth Jacobson, Deb Mapes, Anne Kallem, Estelle Katz, Hannah Reich, Dr. Margot Tallmer, Joyce Kingsboro, Karen Peterson.

To my daughter, Risa Sokolsky, who ferreted out songs from many corners, an added thanks.

And thanks, too, to my dear friend and editor Sheila Barry, whose keen mind, gentle, firm demands and total expertise make the hard work a joyful task.

CONTENTS

Going Buggy   5

The Ants Go Marching • Baby Bumble Bee • The Grasshopper Song • The Flea Fly Song • There Was a Bee-Eye-Ee-Eye-Ee

Ask the Animals   13

Glunk, Glunk, Glunk • Where Is Your Goose? • The Horse Went Around • Six Little Ducks • Little Peter Rabbit • Three Green Speckled Frogs • I Had a Rooster

Snacktime!   25

The Duchess at Tea • The Prune Song • The Quartermaster Corps • The Peanut Butter Song • On Top of My Pizza • The Swiss Cheese Song • Three Ways to Get Peanut Butter Off the Roof of Your Mouth • Gum Song • Birds in the Wilderness • I Want a Chocolate Malted

Kooky Characters   37

Old Mother Leary • Dirty Bill • Clementine • Sweet Rosie O'Grady • Arabella Miller • Old Joe Clarke • Old Mrs. Lazibones • Christopher McCracken • Lulabel

The Best of the Beasts   51

Five Little Monkeys • The Little Skunk Hole • The Smile on the Crocodile • The Bear Song • Pop Goes the Weasel • Fuzzy Wuzzy

Completely Crazy   61

I Wish I Was • The Alphabet Song • Let's Go Bowling in Bowling Green • A Sailor Went to Sea Sea Sea • Do Your Ears Hang Low? • I'm a Nut • Reuben, Reuben • I Am Slowly Going Crazy • Poor Roger Is Dead

Pure Silliness   71

Ninety-nine Miles from Home • We Don't Want to Go Home • Around the Corner • Three Little Witches • Catch a Wiffer Woffer • The Billboard Song • Mud, Mud, Glorious Mud • One Bottle Pop • The Walloping Windowblind

Can You Top This?   85

There Were Three Jolly Fishermen • The Old Family Toothbrush • There's a Hole in the Bucket • John Jacob Jingleheimer Schmidt • Rise and Shine • The Slithery D

Index of First Lines   95

Index   96

To the memory of Becky Perces . . .
a rare and beautiful person . . .
and such a lovely dancer . . . with love

GOING BUGGY

The Ants Go Marching

To the tune of "When Johnny Comes Marching Home"

The ants go march-ing one by one, hur - rah,_____ hur-rah,_____ The ants go march-ing one by one, hur-rah,_____ hur - rah,_____ The_ ants go march-ing one by one, The lit - tle one stops_ to suck his thumb, And they all go march-ing out in the big pa - rade._____

The Ants Go Marching

The ants go marching one by one, hurrah, hurrah,
The ants go marching one by one, hurrah, hurrah,
The ants go marching one by one,
The little one stops to suck his thumb,
And they all go marching out in the big parade.

The ants go marching two by two, hurrah, hurrah,
The ants go marching two by two, hurrah, hurrah,
The ants go marching two by two,
The little one stops to tie his shoe,
And they all go marching out in the big parade.

The ants go marching three by three, hurrah, hurrah,
The ants go marching three by three, hurrah, hurrah,
The ants go marching three by three,
The little one stops to climb a tree,
And they all go marching out in the big parade.

The ants go marching four by four, hurrah, hurrah,
The ants go marching four by four, hurrah, hurrah,
The ants go marching four by four,
The little one stops to sleep some more,
And they all go marching out in the big parade.

The ants go marching five by five, hurrah, hurrah,
The ants go marching five by five, hurrah, hurrah,
The ants go marching five by five,
The little one stops to joke and jive,
And they all go marching out in the big parade.

The ants go marching six by six, hurrah, hurrah,
The ants go marching six by six, hurrah, hurrah,
The ants go marching six by six,
The little one stops to do some tricks,
And they all go marching out in the big parade.

The ants go marching seven by seven, hurrah, hurrah,
The ants go marching seven by seven, hurrah, hurrah,
The ants go marching seven by seven,
The little one stops to point to heaven,
And they all go marching out in the big parade.

The ants go marching eight by eight, hurrah, hurrah,
The ants go marching eight by eight, hurrah, hurrah,
The ants go marching eight by eight,
The little one stops to shut the gate,
And they all go marching out in the big parade.

The ants go marching nine by nine, hurrah, hurrah,
The ants go marching nine by nine, hurrah, hurrah,
The ants go marching nine by nine,
The little one stops to read a sign,
And they all go marching out in the big parade.

The ants go marching ten by ten, hurrah, hurrah,
The ants go marching ten by ten, hurrah, hurrah,
The ants go marching ten by ten,
The little one stops to say "THE END,"
And they all go marching out in the big parade.

Baby Bumble Bee

To the tune of "Arkansas Traveller"

Oh, I'm bring-ing home a ba - by bum - ble bee, Won't my mom - my

be so proud of me, 'Cause I'm bring - ing home a ba - by

bum - ble bee— Buz - zy, buz - zy, buz - zy— *(Spoken)* **OOOOH, it bit me!**

Baby Bumble Bee

Oh, I'm bringing home a baby bumble
    bee,
Won't my mommy be so proud of me,
'Cause I'm bringing home a baby bum-
    ble bee—
Buzzy, buzzy, buzzy—
(*spoken*) OOOOH, it bit me!

Oh, I'm bringing home a baby rattle-
    snake,
Won't my mommy shi—ver and shake,
'Cause I'm bringing home a baby rattle-
    snake—
Rattle, rattle, rattle—
(*spoken*) OOOOH, it bit me!

Oh, I'm bringing home a baby tur-tle,
Won't my mommy really pop her girdle,
'Cause I'm bringing home a baby
    tur-tle—
Snappy, snappy, snappy—
(*spoken*) OOOOH, it bit me!

Oh, I'm bringing home a baby dinosaur,
Won't my mommy fall right through the
    floor,
'Cause I'm bringing home a baby dino-
    saur—
Gobble, gobble, gobble—
(*spoken*) OOOOH, it ate me!

The Grasshopper Song

The Grasshopper Song

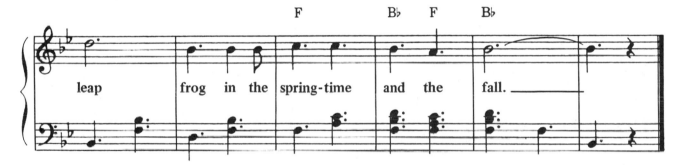

To the same tune:
The Flea Fly Song

The first grasshopper jumped right
   over the second grasshopper's back.
Oh, the first grasshopper jumped right
   over the second grasshopper's back.
The first grasshopper jumped right over
   the second grasshopper's back.
Oh, the first grasshopper jumped right
   over the second grasshopper's back.

Chorus
They were only playing leap frog,
They were only playing leap frog,
They were only playing leap frog,
In the springtime and the fall.

One flea fly flew up the flu and
   the other flea fly flew down.
Oh, one flea fly flew up the flu
   and the other flea fly flew down.
Oh, one flea fly flew up the flu and
   the other flea fly flew down.
Oh, one flea fly flew up the flu
   and the other flea fly flew down.

Chorus
They were only playing flu fly,
They were only playing flu fly,
They were only playing flu fly
In the springtime and the fall.

There Was a Bee-Eye-Ee-Eye-Ee

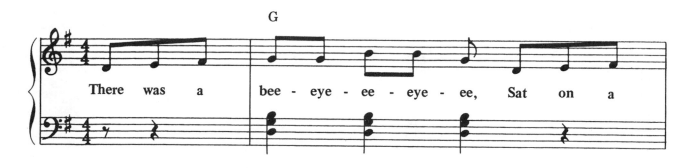

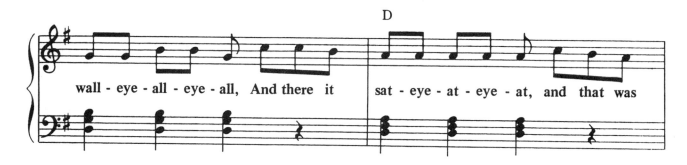

There was a bee-eye-ee-eye-ee,
Sat on a wall-eye-all-eye-all,
And there he sat-eye-at-eye-at,
And that was all-eye-all-eye-all.

Then came a boy-eye-oy-eye-oy,
Who had a stick-eye-ick-eye-ick,
And gave that bee-eye-ee-eye-ee
An awful lick-eye-ick-eye-ick.

And so that bee-eye-ee-eye-ee
Began to sting-eye-ing-eye-ing
And hurt that boy-eye-oy-eye-oy
Like anything-eye-ing-eye-ing!

And then that boy-eye-oy-eye-oy
Let out a yell-eye-ell-eye-ell
And told that bee-eye-ee-eye-ee
To go someplace I will not tell.

And then that bee-eye-ee-eye-ee
Gave one big cough-eye-off-eye-off,
And one last smile-eye-ile-eye-ile,
And he buzzed off-eye-off-eye-off.

12

ASK THE ANIMALS

Glunk, Glunk, Glunk

"Ba-rump," went the little green frog.
"Ba-rump," went the little green frog.
"Ba-rump," went the little green frog
        one day,
And his eyes went, "Glunk, glunk, glunk!"

Where Is Your Goose?

Su - sie, oh, Su - sie, Oh, where is your goose? She's

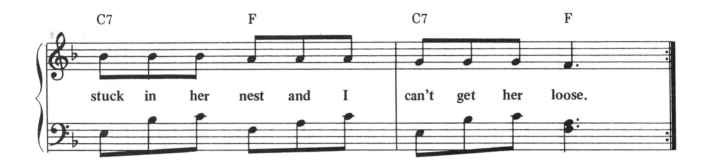

stuck in her nest and I can't get her loose.

Susie, oh, Susie,
Oh, where is your goose?
She's stuck in her nest
And I can't get her loose.

Johnny, oh, Johnny,
Oh, where is your cat?
He's lost in the cellar
And that—is that.

Freddie, oh, Freddie,
Oh, where is your hog?
He got cut in pork chops
And fed to the dog.

Cindy, oh, Cindy,
Where's your water snake?
He's hugged, and he's kissed,
And he's thrown in the lake.

Teddie, oh, Teddie,
Oh, where is your goat?
He's down at the pool
Where he's learning to float.

Linda, oh, Linda,
Oh, where is your pig?
He's gone to the store
To pick up a new wig.

Norman, oh, Norman,
Oh, where is your frog?
I bought him some sneakers
And taught him to jog.

Debbie, oh, Debbie,
Oh, where is your fish?
Right there in the oven—
He's baked in a dish.

Steven, oh, Steven,
Oh, where is your mouse?
He's eating Swiss cheese
In a trap in the house.

Shirley, oh, Shirley,
Oh, where is your duck?
He's off at the races
And trying his luck.

The Horse Went Around

To the tune of "Turkey in the Straw"

Oh, the horse went a - rou - nd With his foot off the ground. Oh, the

horse went a - rou - nd With his foot off the ground. Oh, the

horse went a - rou - nd With his foot off the ground. Oh, the

CHORUS (spoken)

horse went a - rou - nd With his foot off the ground. Next verse,

same as the first, a lit - tle bit loud - er and a lit - tle bit worse!

The Horse Went Around

Oh, the horse went around
With his foot off the ground.
Oh, the horse went around
With his foot off the ground.
Oh, the horse went around
With his foot off the ground.
Oh, the horse went around
With his foot off the ground.

Chorus

(*spoken*) Next verse
           Same as the first.
           A little bit louder
           And a little bit worse.

Oh, the horse went around
With his foot off the _____ .
Oh, the horse went around
With his foot off the _____ .
Oh, the horse went around
With his foot off the _____ .
Oh, the horse went around
With his foot off the _____ .

Chorus

Oh, the horse went around
With his foot off _____ .
Oh, the horse went around
With his foot off _____ .
Oh, the horse went around
With his foot off _____ .
Oh, the horse went around
With his foot off _____ .

Chorus

Sing the song nine times, leaving out the
last word each time, so that finally you're
singing in total silence. After this, sing
the entire song aloud once more.

Six Little Ducks

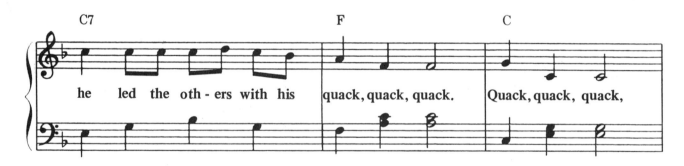

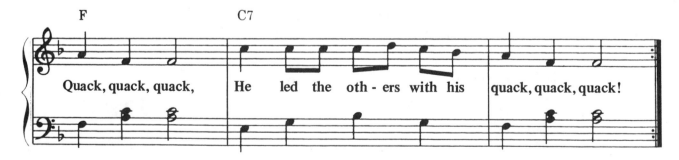

Six little ducks
That I once knew,
Fat ones, skinny ones,
Fair ones, too.
But the one little duck
With a feather on its back,
He led the others
With a quack, quack, quack.

Quack, quack, quack,
Quack, quack, quack.
He led the others
With a quack, quack, quack!

Down to the river they would go,
Wibble, wobble, wibble, wobble to and fro.

Six Little Ducks

Home from the river they would come,
Wibble, wobble, wibble, wobble,
Right back home.

Quack, quack, quack,
Quack, quack, quack,
Right back home
With a quack, quack, quack!

• • • • • • • • • • • • • •

Little Peter Rabbit

To the tune of "Battle Hymn of the Republic"

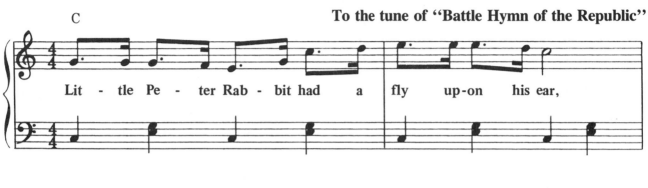

Lit - tle Pe - ter Rab - bit had a fly up-on his ear,

Lit - tle Pe - ter Rab - bit had a fly up-on his ear,

Lit - tle Pe - ter Rab - bit had a fly up - on his ear and he

flicked it till it flew a - way.

Little Peter Rabbit

Little Peter Rabbit had a fly upon his
  ear,
Little Peter Rabbit had a fly upon his
  ear,
Little Peter Rabbit had a fly upon his
  ear,
And he flicked it till it flew away!

Little Peter Rabbit had a fly upon his
  _____ ,
Little Peter Rabbit had a fly upon his
  _____ ,
Little Peter Rabbit had a fly upon his
  _____ ,
And he flicked it till it flew away.

Little Peter Rabbit had a _____ upon
  his _____ ,
Little Peter Rabbit had a _____ upon
  his _____ ,
Little Peter Rabbit had a _____ upon
  his _____ ,
And he flicked it till it flew away.

Little Peter _____ had a _____ upon
  his _____ ,
Little Peter _____ had a _____ upon
  his _____ ,
Little Peter _____ had a _____ upon
  his _____ ,
And he flicked it till it flew away.

Little _____   _____ had a
  _____ upon his _____ ,
Little _____   _____ had a
  _____ upon his _____ ,
Little _____   _____ had a
  _____ upon his _____ ,
And he flicked it till it flew away.

● ● ● ● ● ● ● ● ● ● ● ● ● ●

Three Green Speckled Frogs

Three green speckled frogs
Sat on a speckled log,
Eating some most delicious bugs,
(*spoken*) YUM YUM.

One jumped into the pool
Where it was nice and cool.
Then there were two green speckled
  frogs.

Two green speckled frogs
Sat on the speckled log,
Eating some most delicious bugs,
(*spoken*) YUM YUM.

One jumped into the pool
Where it was nice and cool.
Then there was one green speckled
  frog.

Three Green Speckled Frogs

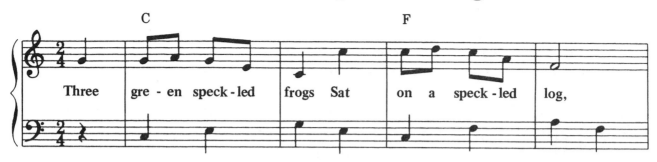

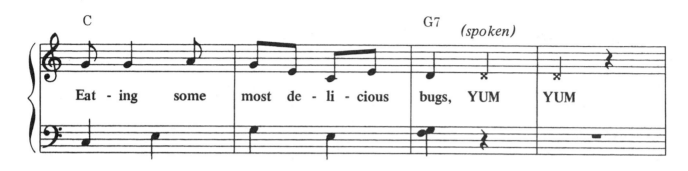

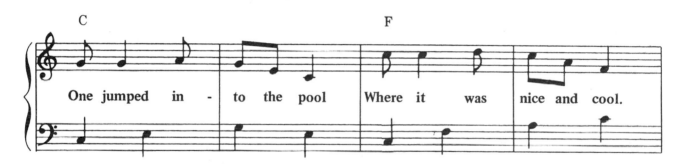

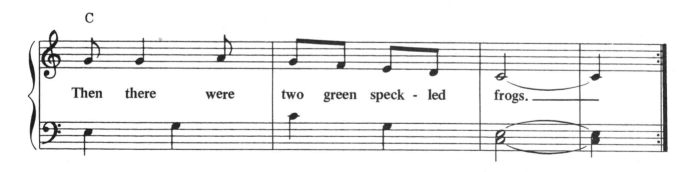

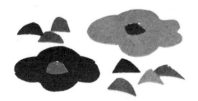

One green speckled frog
Sat on a speckled log,
Eating some most delicious bugs,
(*spoken*) YUM YUM.
He jumped into the pool
Where it was nice and cool,
Then there were no green speckled frogs.

I Had a Rooster

This is an add-on song. Each time you sing a new verse, you add on all the animals that went before, ending with the little rooster.

I Had a Rooster

I Had a Rooster

I had a rooster and the rooster pleased
   me,
I fed my rooster on a greenberry tree.
The little rooster went, "Cock-a-doodle
   doo,
Dee doodle-dee, doodle-dee, doodle-dee
   doo."

I had a cat and the cat pleased me,
I fed my cat on a greenberry tree.
The little cat went, (*spoken*), "Meow,
   meow,"
The little rooster went, "Cock-a-doodle
   doo,
Dee doodle-dee, doodle-dee, doodle-dee
   doo."

Go on to more verses:

I had a pig ("oink, oink, oink")
I had a cow ("mooo, mooo")
I had a duck ("quack, quack, quack")
I had a lion ("roar, roar")
I had a baby ("waagh, waagh")

You don't have to stick with animals or
humans. You can make up your own
verses using anything you want. You
could try:

   clocks ("tick, tick-tock")
   trains ("choo, choo, choo")
   cars ("beep, beep, beep")
   musical instruments such as horns
      ("toot, toot, toot") or
      guitars ("plunk, plunk, plunk")
   or even computers ("blip, blip, blip")

and you can vary the sound effects.

SNACKTIME!

The Duchess at Tea

I sat next to the Duchess at tea.
It was just as I thought it would be.
Her rum-bl-ings ab-dom-in-al
Were sim-pl-y phen-om-en-al,
Everyone thought it was me!

The Prune Song

The Quartermaster Corps

Oh, it's beans, beans, beans,
That turn us into fiends
In the corps, in the corps.
Oh, it's beans, beans, beans,
That turn us into fiends,
In the Quartermaster Corps.

Chorus
Mine eyes are dim;
I cannot see.
I have not brought my specs with me.

Oh, it's soup, soup, soup,
That knocks you for a loop
In the corps, in the corps,
Oh, it's soup, soup, soup
That knocks you for a loop
In the Quartermaster Corps.

Chorus

Oh, it's cheese, cheese, cheese,
That brings you to your knees
In the corps, in the corps. (*Repeat*)

Chorus

Oh, it's cake, cake, cake,
That makes your stomach ache
In the corps, in the corps. (*Repeat*)

Chorus

Oh, it's pie, pie, pie,
That hits you in the eye
In the corps, in the corps. (*Repeat*)

Chorus

Oh, it's meat, meat, meat,
That isn't fit to eat
In the corps, in the corps. (*Repeat*)

Chorus

Oh, it's peas, peas, peas,
That make you want to sneeze
In the corps, in the corps. (*Repeat*)

Chorus

Oh, it's stew, stew, stew,
That turns you black and blue
In the corps, in the corps. (*Repeat*)

Chorus

Oh, it's bread, bread, bread,
Sits in your gut like lead
In the corps, in the corps. (*Repeat*)

Chorus

Oh, it's pears, pears, pears,
That give you curly hairs
In the corps, in the corps. (*Repeat*)

Chorus

The Quartermaster Corps

Oh, it's beans, beans, beans, that turn us in-to fiends, In the corps, _____ in the corps, _____ Oh, it's beans, beans, beans, that turns us in-to fiends, in the Quar-ter-mas-ter Corps. _____

CHORUS

Mine eyes are dim, I can-not see, I have not brought my specs with me.

The Peanut Butter Song

CHORUS

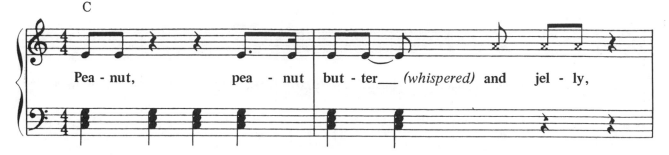

Pea - nut, pea - nut but - ter __ *(whispered)* and jel - ly,

Pea - nut, pea - nut but - ter __ *(whispered)* and jel - ly. You

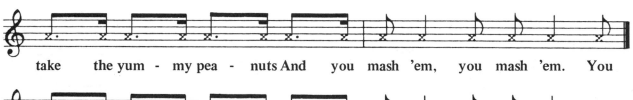

take the yum - my pea - nuts And you mash 'em, you mash 'em. You

take the yum - my pea - nuts And you mash 'em, you mash 'em.

You take the peanut butter
And you spread it, you spread it.
You take the peanut butter
And you spread it, you spread it.

Chorus

Then you take the grapes
and you squish 'em, you squish 'em.
Then you take the grapes
And you squish 'em, you squish 'em.

Chorus

Then you take the jelly
And you spread it, you spread it.
Then you take the jelly
And you spread it, you spread it.

You take the peanut butter and jelly
And put them together, put them together.
You take the peanut butter and jelly
And put them together, put them together.

Chorus

Then you take that knife
And you cut it, you cut it,
Then you take that knife
And you cut it, you cut it.

Chorus

Then you take the sandwich
And you eat it, you eat it.
Then you take the sandwich
And you eat it, you eat it.

The Peanut Butter Song

Hum the chorus three or four or five times more and more quietly, until fadeout, chewing.

● ● ● ● ● ● ● ● ● ● ● ● ●

On Top of My Pizza

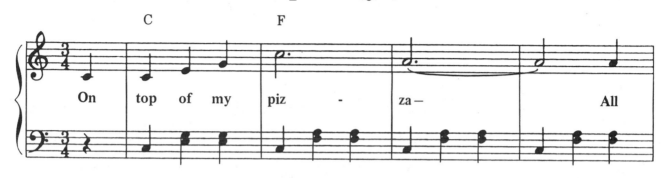

On top of my piz - za— All

cov - ered with sauce, _____ Could not find the

mush - rooms, _____ I think they got lost. _____

On top of my pizza—
All covered with sauce—
Could not find the mushrooms,
I think they got lost.

I looked in the closet,
I looked in the sink,
I looked in the cup that
Held my cola drink.

I looked in the saucepan,
Right under the lid,
No matter where I looked,
Those mushrooms stayed hid.

Next time you make pizza,
I'm begging you, please,
Do not give me mushrooms,
But just plain old cheese.

The Swiss Cheese Song

Lyrics under the staves:

There once was a wom - an who gob - bled Swiss cheese,

Gob - bled Swiss cheese, gob - bled Swiss cheese, And

one day she woke up with holes in her knees,

Woke up with holes in her knees. . . . ____

There once was a woman who gobbled
    Swiss cheese,
Gobbled Swiss cheese, gobbled Swiss
    cheese,
And one day she woke up with holes in
    her knees,
Woke up with holes in her knees. . . .

This woman cried, "Help me, oh, what
    can I do?
What can I do? What can I do?
When I look at my knees I see sky
    shining through.
Now I see sky shining through."

The Swiss Cheese Song

She ran to the doctor who answered
with ease,
Answered with ease, answered with
ease,
"Just swallow some tiddlywinks.
They'll fill up your knees.
Tiddlywinks will fill up your knees."

She salted some tiddlywinks and gob-
bled down lots,
Gobbled down lots, gobbled down lots.
Now 'stead of holes, she's got green
polka dots,
Now she's got green polka dots.

Three Ways to Get Peanut Butter
Off the Roof of Your Mouth

There are three ways to get peanut
butter off the roof of your
mouth.
One way is to shake your head back
and forth
(*shake head vigorously*).
If that doesn't work
you could kind of whistle
(*whistle*).

If this doesn't work, you could scrape it
off with your first finger
(*scrape it off*).

There are three ways to get peanut
butter off your finger.
One way is to shake it off
(*shake finger vigorously*).
Another way is to blow it off
(*try that*).
If that doesn't work, you can scrape it
off with your two front teeth
(*do it*).

There are three ways to get peanut
butter off the roof of your
mouth (*and so on*).

Gum Song

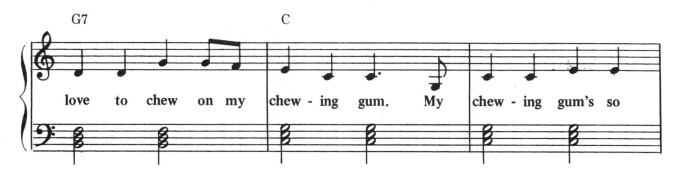

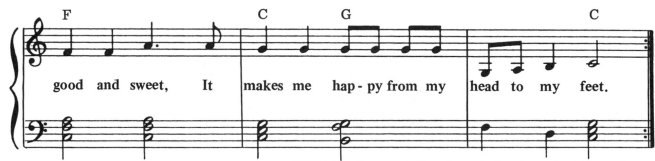

Chomp chomp, nibble nibble, yum,
    yum, yum,
I love to chew on my chewing gum.
My chewing gum's so good and sweet,
It makes me happy from my head to my
    feet.

I love to pull my gum out far
And pluck it like a big guitar.
I wind it around my thumb with care,
'Cause nobody likes it when it gets in
    your hair.

Blowing a bubble's mighty tough,
You've got to stick your tongue out
    enough.
Now I'm ready, just look at me
And I'll blow you a bubble as big as a
    tree.

Sometimes when I'm chewing gum
I make it flat with the top of my tongue.
I make it flat, then I take it out
And it makes a map of the top of my
    mouth.

My gum makes pops and cracks and
    clicks
Against my teeth and against my lips.
When I'm all alone, no one else around,
I love to hear that chewing gum sound.

Chomp chomp, nibble nibble, yum,
    yum, yum,
I love to chew on my chewing gum.
My chewing gum's so good and sweet,
It makes me happy from my head to my
    feet.

34

Birds in the Wilderness

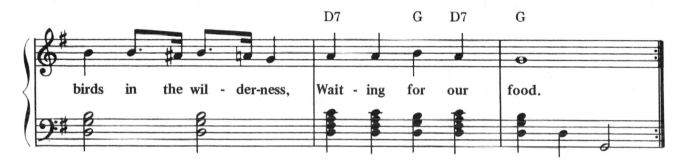

Here we sit like birds in the wilderness,
Birds in the wilderness,
Birds in the wilderness,
Here we sit like birds in the wilderness,
Waiting for our food.

Here we sit like birds in the wilderness,
Birds in the wilderness,
Birds in the wilderness,
Here we sit like birds in the wilderness,
Waiting for our soup.

Here we sit like birds in the wilderness,
Birds in the wilderness,
Birds in the wilderness,
Here we sit like birds in the wilderness,
Waiting for our bread.

Here we sit like birds in the wilderness,
Birds in the wilderness,
Birds in the wilderness,
Here we sit like birds in the wilderness,
Waiting for our meat.

Here we sit like birds in the wilderness,
Birds in the wilderness,
Birds in the wilderness,
Here we sit like birds in the wilderness,
Waiting for dessert.

I Want a Chocolate Malted (Round)

The music for this song is actually based on the Grand Fugue from Bach's Toccata in G Minor. It makes a yummy round.

I want—
I want a malted,
I want a chocolate malted,
I want a chocolate malted.

KOOKY CHARACTERS

Old Mother Leary

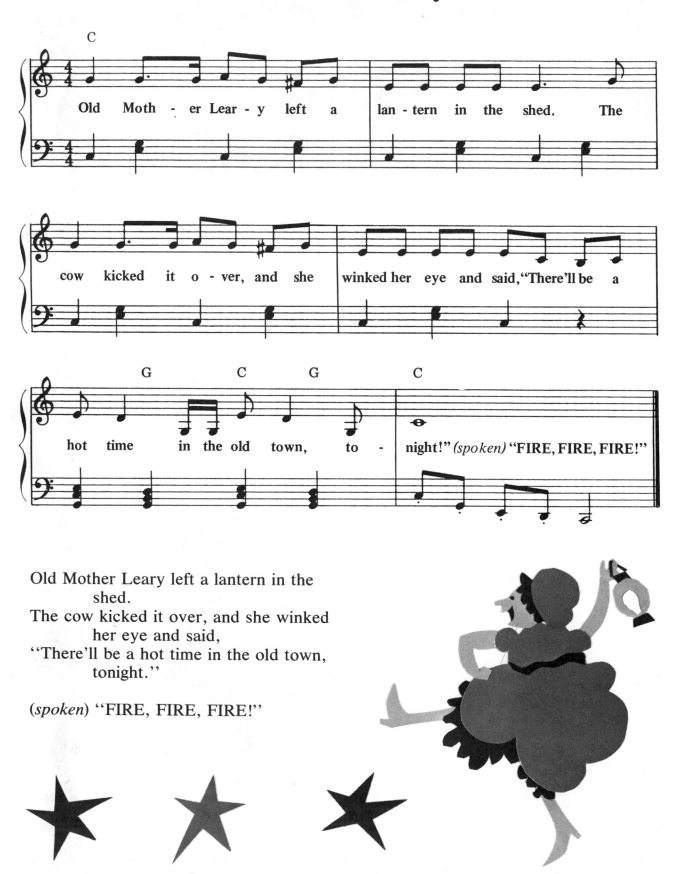

Old Mother Leary left a lantern in the
   shed.
The cow kicked it over, and she winked
   her eye and said,
"There'll be a hot time in the old town,
   tonight."

(*spoken*) "FIRE, FIRE, FIRE!"

38

Dirty Bill

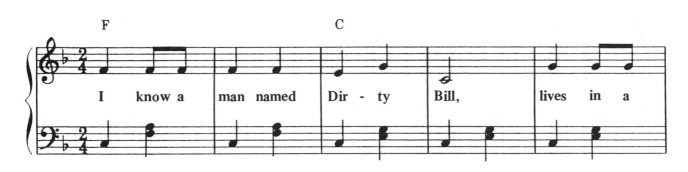

I know a man named Dirty Bill,
Lives in a house on Garbage Hill,
Never took a bath and never will.
Oigh, foigh, Dirty Bill!

Clementine

Clementine

In a cavern, in a canyon,
Excavating for a mine,
Lived a miner forty-niner
And his daughter, Clementine.

Chorus
Oh, my darling, oh, my darling,
Oh, my darling Clementine,
You are lost and gone forever,
Dreadful sorry, Clementine.

Light she was and like a fairy,
And her shoes were number nine,
Herring boxes without topses,
Sandals were for Clementine.

Chorus

Drove her ducklings to the water,
Every morning just at nine,
Hit her foot against a splinter,
Fell into the foaming brine.

Chorus

Ruby lips above the water,
Blowing bubbles soft and fine,
But alas, I was no swimmer
So I lost my Clementine.

Chorus

Then the miner, forty-niner,
Soon began to peak and pine,
Thought he oughta join his daughter,
Now he's with his Clementine.

Chorus

There's a churchyard on the hillside,
Where the flowers grow and twine,
There grow roses, 'mongst the posies,
Fertilized by Clementine.

Chorus

In my dreams she still doth haunt me,
Robed in garlands soaked in brine,
Though in life I used to hug her,
Now she's dead, I draw the line.

Chorus

Now you scouts may learn the moral
Of this little tale of mine,
Artificial respiration
Would have saved my Clementine.

Chorus

How I missed her, how I missed her,
How I missed my Clementine,
Till I kissed her little sister,
And forgot my Clementine.

Chorus

Sweet Rosie O'Grady

Sweet Ros-ie O' Gra - dy, She was a seam-stress by birth.____ She got tir - ed of liv - ing, And de - cid - ed to leave this earth.____ So she ate a tape meas - ure, But dy - ing by inch-es was hard.____ So she went out in the gar - den,____ And lay down and died by the yard.

42

Arabella Miller

Little Arabella Miller
Found a woolly caterpillar.
First it crawled upon her mother,
Then upon her little brother.
They said, "Arabella Miller,
Take away your caterpillar!"

Arabella did not take it.
She decided to forsake it.
So it crawled up on the tree
And fell down on you and me.
Please, dear Arabella Miller,
Take away your caterpillar!

Old Joe Clarke

Old Joe Clarke's a fine old man,
Tell you the reason why.
He keeps good candy round his house
And lots of apple pie.

Chorus Fare ye well, Old Joe Clarke,
Fare ye well, I say,
Fare ye well, Old Joe Clarke,
I'm a-goin' away.

44

Old Joe Clarke

Old Joe Clarke had a house
Fifteen stories high,
And every story in that house
Was filled with chicken pie.

Chorus

I went down to Old Joe's house,
Never been there before.
He slept on the feather bed
And I slept on the floor.

Chorus

Old Joe Clarke had a cow,
She was long as a rail.
It took a blackbird one whole day
To fly from head to tail!

Chorus

Old Joe Clarke had a mule,
His name was Morgan Brown.
And every tooth in that mule's head
Was sixteen inches round.

Chorus

Old Joe Clarke had a cat—
She was fat and mean.
She stuck her head in the buttermilk jar
And washed her whiskers clean.

Chorus

I went down to Old Joe's house—
He invited me to supper.
I stubbed my toe on the table leg
And stuck my nose in the butter.

Chorus

Old Mrs. Lazibones

Old Mis - sus La - zi - bones And her dirt - y daugh - ter

Nev - er used soap And nev - er used __ wa - ter.

CHORUS

Hig - gle - dy pig - gle - dy cow - pat,

What d' you think of that?

Old Mrs. Lazibones

Old Mrs. Lazibones
And her dirty daughter
Never used soap
And never used water.

Chorus   Higgledy piggledy cowpat,
What d'you think of that?

Daisies from their fingernails,
Birds' nests in their hair-O,
Dandelions from their ears,
What a dirty pair-O!

Chorus

Came a prince who sought a bride,
Riding past their doorstep,
"Quick," said Mrs. Lazibones.
"Girl, under the water tap."

Chorus

Washed her up and washed her down,
Then she washed her sideways,
But the prince was far, far away,
He'd ridden off on the highways.

Chorus

Christopher McCracken

To the tune of "Battle Hymn of the Republic"

Chris-to-pher Mc-Crack-en went a-fish-ing for some crabs,

Chris-to-pher Mc-Crack-en went a-fish-ing for some crabs,

Chris-to-pher Mc-Crack-en went a-fish-ing for some

crabs, But he did-n't catch a *(clap, clap)* crab. Oh,

all ___ he caught was some old vi-rus, all ___ he

Christopher McCracken

B♭

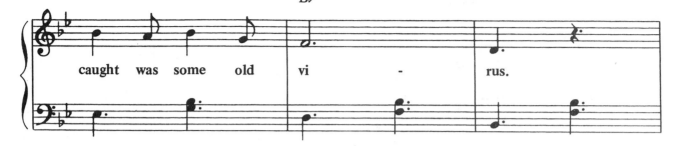

caught was some old vi - rus.

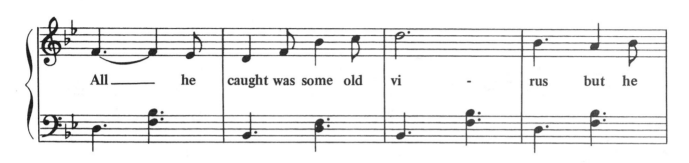

All ____ he caught was some old vi - rus but he

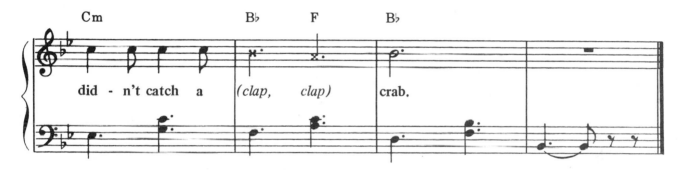

Cm   B♭   F   B♭

did - n't catch a *(clap, clap)* crab.

Christopher McCracken went a-fishing
    for some crabs,
Christopher McCracken went a-fishing
    for some crabs,
Christopher McCracken went a-fishing
    for some crabs,
But he didn't catch a *(clap, clap)* crab.

Oh, all he caught was some old virus,
All he caught was some old virus,
All he caught was some old virus,
But he didn't catch a *(clap, clap)* crab.

Lulabel

(Spoken in falsetto voice)
**OH MY GOODNESS!
OH MY SOUL!
THERE GOES LULABEL
DOWN THE HOLE!**

THE BEST OF THE BEASTS

Five Little Monkeys

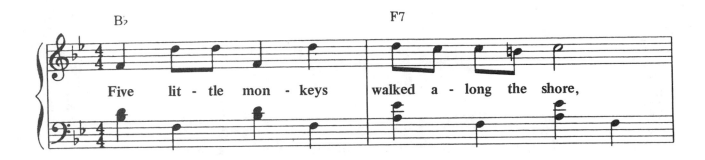

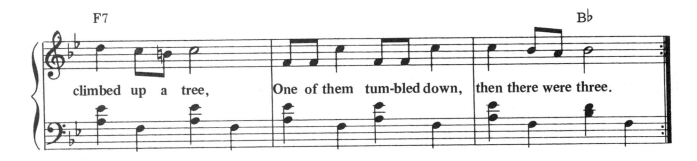

Five little monkeys walked along the
    shore,
One went sailing,
Then there were four.

Four little monkeys climbed up a tree,
One of them tumbled down,
Then there were three.

Three little monkeys found a pot of glue,
One got stuck in it,
Then there were two.

Two little monkeys found a raisin bun,
One ran away with it,
Then there was one.

One little monkey, red in the face,
They trained him as an astronaut
And sent him out in space.

The Little Skunk Hole

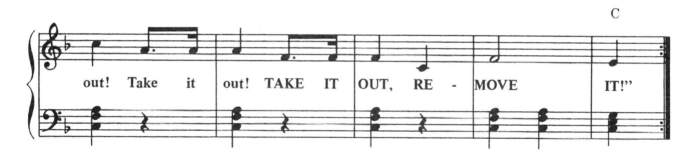

Oh, I stuck my head
In the little skunk hole,
And the little skunk said,
"Well, bless my soul!
Take it out! Take it out! Take it out!
    TAKE IT OUT!
    REMOVE IT!"

Well, I didn't take it out,
And the little skunk said,
"If you don't take it out,
You'll wish you were dead.
Take it out! Take it out! Take it out!
(*holding nose*) Pee-yoo! I removed it
(*spoken*) TOOOO LATE!!!!!!!!!!

The Smile on the Crocodile

She sailed away on a sunny summer day
On the back of a crocodile.
"You see," said she,
"He's as tame as he can be—
I'll ride him down the Nile."

The Smile on the Crocodile

croc winked his eye, As she bade them all good - bye,

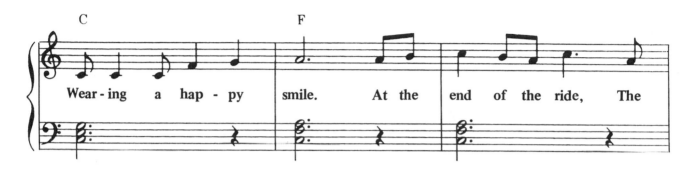

Wear - ing a hap - py smile. At the end of the ride, The

la - dy was in - side, And the smile on the croc - o - dile.

The croc winked his eye
As she bade them all good-bye,
Wearing a happy smile.
At the end of the ride,
The lady was inside
And the smile on the crocodile!

The Bear Song

The other day	He looked at me
(the other day)	(he looked at me),
I saw a bear	I looked at him
(I saw a bear),	(I looked at him),
A great big bear	He sized up me
(a great big bear)	(he sized up me),
A-way up there	I sized up him
(a-way up there),	(I sized up him),
The other day I saw a bear,	He looked at me, I looked at him,
A great big bear a-way up there.	He sized up me, I sized up him.

The Bear Song

He said to me
  (he said to me),
"Why don't you run?
  (Why don't you run?)
I see you ain't
  (I see you ain't)
Got any gun."
  (got any gun)
He said to me, "Why don't you run?
I see you ain't got any gun."

And so I ran
  (and so I ran)
Away from there
  (away from there),
And right behind
  (and right behind)
Me was that bear
  (me was that bear),
And so I ran away from there,
And right behind me was that bear.

In front of me
  (in front of me)
There was a tree
  (there was a tree),
A great big tree
  (a great big tree),
Oh, golly gee
  (oh, golly gee),
In front of me there was a tree,
A great big tree, oh, golly gee.

The nearest branch
  (the nearest branch)
Was ten feet up
  (was ten feet up),
I had to jump
  (I had to jump)
And trust my luck
  (and trust my luck),
The nearest branch was ten feet up,
I had to jump and trust my luck.

And so I jumped
  (and so I jumped)
Into the air
  (into the air),
And missed that branch
  (and missed that branch)
Away up there
  (away up there),
And so I jumped into the air,
And missed that branch away up there.

Now don't you fret
  (now don't you fret)
And don't you frown
  (and don't you frown),
I caught that branch
  (I caught that branch)
On the way back down
  (on the way back down)
Now don't you fret and don't you frown
I caught that branch on the way back
      down.

That's all there is
  (that's all there is)
There ain't no more
  (there ain't no more),
Until I meet
  (until I meet)
That bear once more
  (that bear once more),
That's all there is, there ain't no more,
Until I meet that bear once more.

The end the end
  (the end the end)
The end the end
  (the end the end),
The end the end
  (the end the end)
The end the end
  (the end the end),
The end the end the end the end,
This time it really is the end.

Pop Goes the Weasel!

All around the cobbler's bench,
The monkey chased the weasel.
The monkey thought 'twas all in fun,
Pop—goes the weasel!
Johnny's got the whooping cough
And Mary's got the measles,
That's the way the money goes,
Pop—goes the weasel!

A penny for a spool of thread,
A penny for a needle,
That's the way the money goes,
Pop—goes the weasel!
You may try to sew and sew
And never make anything regal
So roll it up and let it go,
Pop—goes the weasel!

Pop Goes the Weasel!

A painter would his lover to paint,
He stood before the easel.
The monkey jumped all over the paint,
Pop—goes the weasel!
When his sweetheart she did laugh,
His temper got so lethal,
He tore the painting up in half,
Pop—goes the weasel!

My son and I went to the fair,
We saw a lot of people.
We spent a lot of money there,
Pop—goes the weasel!
I got sick from all the sun,
My sonny boy got the measles.
Still we had a lot of fun,
Pop—goes the weasel!

I climbed up and down the coast
To find a golden eagle.
I climbed the rocks and thought I was
        close,
Pop—goes the weasel!
But, alas, I lost my way,
Saw nothing but a seagull,
I tore my pants and killed the day,
Pop—goes the weasel!

I went to the grocery store,
I thought a little cheese'll
Be good to catch a mouse on the floor,
Pop—goes the weasel!
But the mouse was very bright
He wasn't a mouse to wheedle,
He took the cheese and said, "Good-
        night,"
Pop—goes the weasel!

Up and down the City Road,
In and out the Eagle,
That's the way the money goes,
Pop—goes the weasel!
Half a pound of tuppenny rice,
Half a pound of treacle,
Mix it up and make it nice,
Pop—goes the weasel!

Every night when I go out,
The monkey's on the table,
Take a stick and knock it off,
Pop—goes the weasel!
Put some pepper on its nose,
And you'll make it sneeze-l,
Catch it fast before it snaps—
Pop—goes the weasel!

A penny for a cotton ball,
A penny for a needle,
That's the way the money goes,
Pop—goes the weasel!
If you want to buy a pig,
Buy a pig with hairs on,
Every hair a penny a pair,
Pop—goes the weasel!

All around the cobbler's bench,
The monkey chased the weasel.
The monkey thought 'twas all in fun,
Pop—goes the weasel!
I've no time to wait and sigh,
I've no time to tease-l,
Kiss me quick—I'm off—goodbye!
Pop—goes the weasel!

Fuzzy Wuzzy

Fuzzy Wuzzy was a bear,
Fuzzy Wuzzy had no hair.
Fuzzy Wuzzy wasn't fuzzy,
No, by gosh, he wasn't, wuzz he?

COMPLETELY CRAZY

I Wish I Was

I Wish I Was

I wish I was
  a ranasasorius,
  a re-papa-tame-eye-ee—
  ha-ha-ha-ha.
But since I am not
And never can hope to be
  a ranasasorius,

  a re-papa-tame-eye-ee—
I'm a June bug,
I'm a turtle,
And I love to hit my head against the
  wall.
  Click Click
(*click your tongue twice*)

● ● ● ● ● ● ● ● ● ● ● ● ● ●

The Alphabet Song

B	ay	bay		C	ay	say	
B	ee	bee		C	ee	see	
B	eye	bye		C	eye	sigh	
Bay	bee	bye		Say	see	sigh	
B	oh	bo		C	oh	so	
Bay	bee	bye	bo	Say	see	sigh	so
B	you	boo		C	you	sue	
Bay	bee	bye bo boo.		Say	see	sigh so sue.	

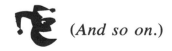 (*And so on.*)

Let's Go Bowling in Bowling Green

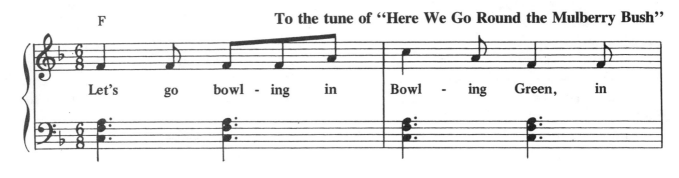

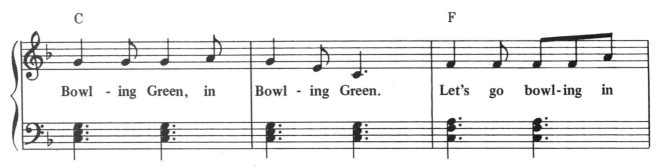

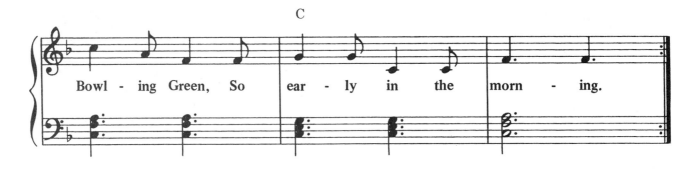

Let's go bowling in Bowling Green,
In Bowling Green, in Bowling Green,
Let's go bowling in Bowling Green,
So early in the morning.

(*spoken*) We can't go bowling in Bowl-
    ing Green,
Why can't we go bowling in Bowling
    Green?
Because of the king.
What king?
Father of the prince.
What prince?

Paw prints—
Handprints—
Fingerprints—
Blueprints—
(*whistle and beckon with finger*) Here,
    Prince, Prince, Prince!

The moral of this story is:
NEVER CONFUSE ASTHMA
    (wheeze)—
WITH PASSION (sigh)!

A Sailor Went to Sea Sea Sea

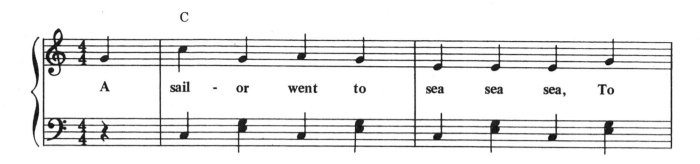

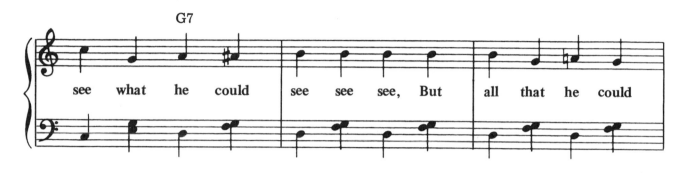

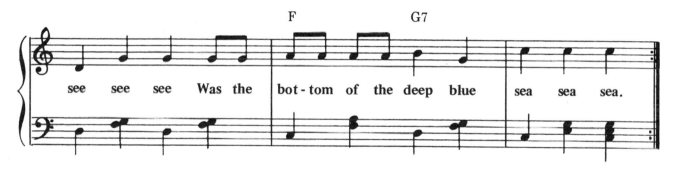

A sailor went to sea sea sea
To see what he could see see see,
But all that he could see see see
Was the bottom of the deep blue sea
    sea sea.

Oh, Helen had a steamboat,
The steamboat had a bell,
When Helen went to heaven
The steamboat went to —

Hello, operator,
Just give me number 9.
If the line is busy
I'll kick your big —

Behind the old piano,
There was a piece of glass,
Helen slipped upon it
And hurt her little —

Ask me for a muffin,
I'll give you some old bread
And if you do not like it,
Just go and soak your head.

Do Your Ears Hang Low?

Do your ears hang low?
Do they wobble to and fro?
Can you tie them in a knot?
Can you tie them in a bow?
Can you toss them over your shoulder
Like a continental soldier?
Do your ears—hang—low?

Yes, my ears hang low.
They can wobble to and fro,
I can tie them in a knot,
I can tie them in a bow,
I can toss them over my shoulder
Like a continental soldier.
Yes, my ears—hang—low.

I'm a Nut

I'm wild about horns on automobiles
That go, "whah ah ah ah ah ah ah ah."
I'm a nut!—Click click—
I'm a pest—Click click—
And the thing I love the best— (*start again.*)

Reuben, Reuben

Reuben, Reuben, I've been thinking,
What the heck have you been drinking?
Looks like water, tastes like wine—
Oh, my gosh, it's turpentine.

I've got a dog; his name is Rover,
He's a very clever pup.
He will stand upon his hind legs,
If you hold his front legs up.

Reuben, Reuben, I've been thinking,
What a silly world this would be,
If the monkeys lived in houses
and we swung from tree to tree.

There's no need to light a night light
On a light night like tonight—
For a night light's light is slight light
When the moonlight's white and bright.

Reuben, Reuben, I've been thinking,
What a funny world this would be,
If jet planes lived in apartments
And we flew across the sea.

I Am Slowly Going Crazy

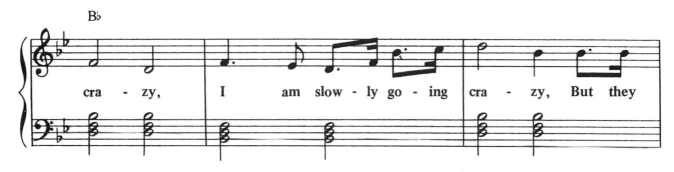

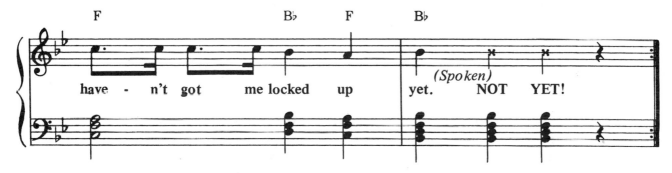

Chorus   I am slowly going crazy,
I am slowly going crazy,
I am slowly going crazy,
But they haven't got me locked up yet!
(*spoken*) NOT YET!

It was midnight on the ocean,
Not a taxi in sight.
The sun was shining brightly,
And it rained all day that night.

Please don't ask me any questions,
I will make no more suggestions.
Please don't ask me any questions,
And I'll tell you no more lies.

Chorus   **Chorus**

Poor Roger Is Dead and Gone to His Grave

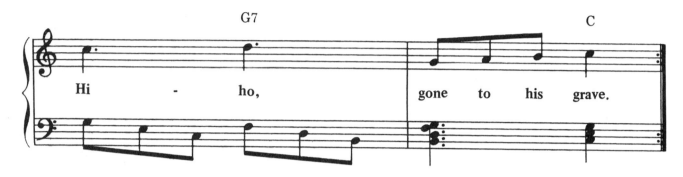

Poor Roger is dead and gone to his
    grave,
Hi-ho, gone to his grave.

There grew an old apple tree over his
    head,
Hi-ho, over his head.

The apples were ripe and ready to fall,
Hi-ho, ready to fall.

There came an old woman, a-picking
        them up,
Hi-ho, a-picking them up.

Old Roger jumped up and he gave her a
        knock,
Hi-ho, gave her a knock.

Which made the old woman go clippety-
        clop,
Hi-ho, clippety-clop.

The saddle and bridle, they lie on the
        shelf,
Hi-ho, lie on the shelf.

If you want any more, you can sing it
        yourself,
Hi-ho, sing it yourself!

PURE SILLINESS

Ninety-nine Miles from Home

Oh, I'm ninety-nine miles from home,
I'm ninety-nine miles from home.
I walk a while, and rest a while,
I'm ninety-nine miles from home.

Oh, I'm ninety-eight miles from home,
I'm ninety-eight miles from home.
I walk a while, and rest a while,
I'm ninety-eight miles from home.

(And so on . . . .)

We Don't Want to Go Home

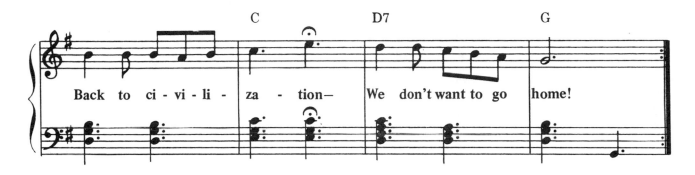

Ten more days of vacation,
Then we go back to the station,
Back to civilization —
We don't want to go home.

We don't want to go home,
We don't want to go home,
We don't want to go home,
We want to stay right here!

Start with ten days of vacation. Then
each day subtract one and sing
the new number of days left.
Finally:

No more days of vacation,
We have to go back to the station,
Back to civilization—
Now we have to go home.

Around the Corner

Around the corner, and under a tree,
A sergeant major once said to me,
"Who would marry you?
I would like to know,

For every time I look at your face,
It makes me want to go
Around the corner," and under a tree

(and on and on and on).

Three Little Witches

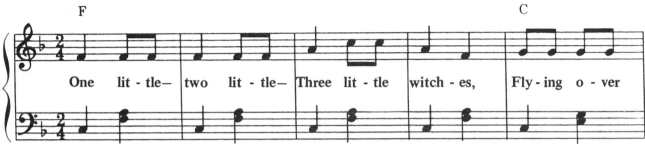

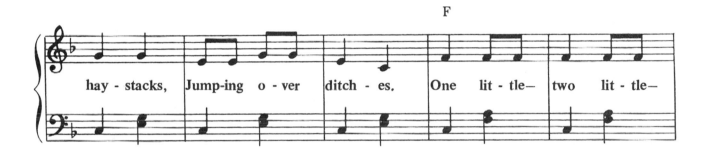

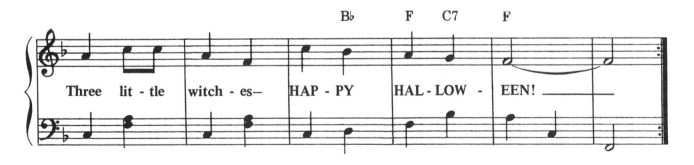

One little—
Two little—
Three little witches,
Flying over haystacks,
Jumping over ditches.
One little—
Two little—
Three little witches—
HAPPY HALLOWEEN!

One little—
Two little—
Three little witches,
Flew over the fence and
Ripped their britches,
Sewed them
Up with fifty stitches—
HAPPY HALLOWEEN!

Catch a Wiffer Woffer

Catch a Wiffer Woffer

Oh, I'm walkin' round the corner
Doing little harm,
Along comes a policeman
And grabs me by the arm.

Oh, he walks me round the corner,
Rings a little bell,
Along comes a wagon,
And knocks me in a cell.

Chorus

I'm singin' eenie meenie and a miney
    moh,
Catch a wiffer woffer by the toe,
And if it hollers, hollers, hollers,
Let it go, I'm singin'
Eenie meenie and a miney moh.

Oh, five o'clock in the morning
I looked up on the wall—
The roaches and the bedbugs
Were having a game of ball.

Oh, the score was six to nothing,
The roaches were ahead—
The bedbugs hit a home run
And knocked me out of bed.

Chorus

Oh, six o'clock in the morning
The jailer comes around,
A piece of bread and coffee
That weighs a half a pound.

Oh, the coffee tastes like tobacco juice,
The bread is hard and stale,
But that's the way they treat the bums
In New York County Jail.

Chorus

I went downtown for breakfast
I ordered ham and eggs.
I ate so many pickles,
The juice ran down my legs.

I fell into a sewer
And that is where I died.
They did not call it murder—
They called it sewer-cide.

Chorus

77

The Billboard Song

ENDING:

As I was walking down the street
One dark and dismal day,
I came upon a billboard
And much to my dismay,
The sign was torn and tattered
From a storm the night before.
The wind and rain had done its job
And this is what I saw:

78

The Billboard Song

Smoke Coca-Cola cigarettes,
Chew Wrigley-Spearmint beer,
And Kennel Ration Dog Food
Makes your wife's complexion clear.
Oh, simonize your baby,
With a Hershey's candy bar,
And Texaco's the beauty cream
That's used by every star.

Please take your next vacation
In a brand new Frigidaire.
And learn to play piano
In your winter underwear.
The doctors say that babies
Should smoke till they are three,
And people in the cities
Ought to bathe in Lipton's Tea—
    with flow-through tea bags!

● ● ● ● ● ● ● ● ● ● ● ● ● ● ●

Mud, Mud, Glorious Mud

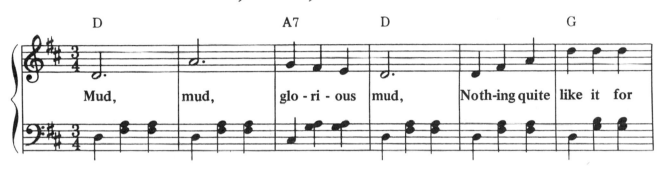

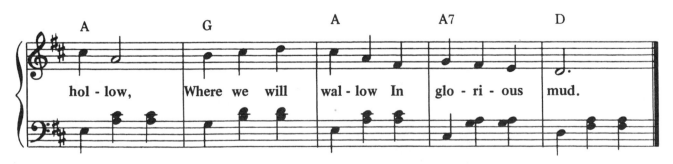

Mud, mud, glorious mud,
Nothing quite like it for cooling your blood.
Follow me, follow,

Down to the hollow,
Where we will wallow
In glorious mud.

One Bottle Pop

One bottle pop,
Two bottle pop,
Three bottle pop,
Four bottle pop,
Five bottle pop,
Six bottle pop,
Seven bottle bottle pop,

Fish and chips and vinegar,
Vinegar, vinegar.
Fish and chips and vinegar.
Pepper pepper pepper salt.

80

One Bottle Pop

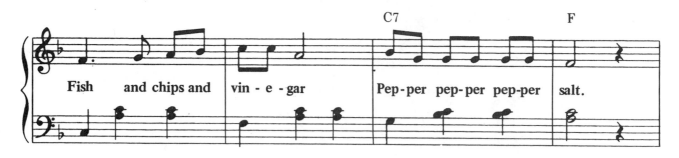

Fish and chips and | vin - e - gar | Pep-per pep-per pep-per | salt.

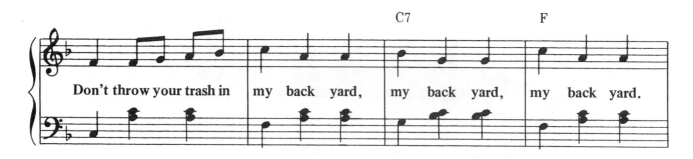

Don't throw your trash in | my back yard, | my back yard, | my back yard.

Don't throw your trash in | my back yard! | My back yard's | full!

Don't throw your trash in my back yard,
My back yard, my back yard
Don't throw your trash in my back yard
My back yard's full!

The Walloping Windowblind

A capital ship for an ocean trip
Was the Walloping Windowblind.
No wind that blew
Dismayed her crew
Nor troubled the captain's mind.
The man at the wheel
Was made to feel
Contempt for the wildest blow-oh-oh,
Though it often appeared
When the gale had cleared
That he'd been in his bunk below.

Chorus
Then blow ye winds heigh-ho
A-roving I will go.
I'll stay no more
On England's shore
So let the music play-ay-ay—
I'm off on the morning train
I'll sail the raging main.
I'm off to my love
With a boxing glove
Ten thousand miles away.

The captain's mate was very sedate,
Yet fond of amusement, too.
He played hopscotch
With the starboard watch,
While the captain tickled the crew.
The gunner we had was apparently
mad,
For he sat on the after rail-ail-ail—
And fired salutes with the captain's
boots
In the teeth of the raging gale.

Chorus

The captain sat on the commodore's hat
And dined in a royal way
On snails and eels and cockatoo heels
And pickled figs each day.
The cook was new and burned the
stew,
So the diet he served the crew
Was a couple of tons of hot cross buns
Served up with sugar and glue.

Chorus

The Walloping Windowblind

The Walloping Windowblind

CAN YOU TOP THIS?

There Were Three Jolly Fishermen

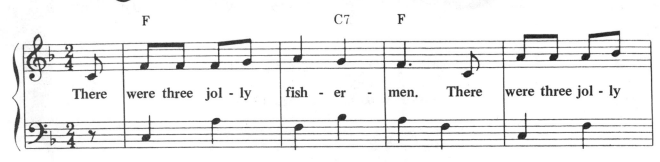

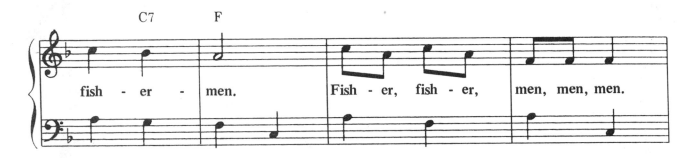

There were three jolly fishermen,
There were three jolly fishermen,
Fisher, fisher, men, men, men.
Fisher, fisher, men, men, men.
There were three jolly fishermen.

The first one's name was Abraham.
The first one's name was Abraham.
Abra, Abra, ham, ham, ham.
Abra, Abra, ham, ham, ham.
The first one's name was Abraham.

The next one's name was Isaac.
The next one's name was Isaac.
I, I, zic, zic, zic.
I, I, zic, zic, zic.
The next one's name was Isaac.

The third one's name was Jacob.
The third one's name was Jacob.
Jay, Jay, cub, cub, cub.
Jay, Jay, cub, cub, cub.
The third one's name was Jacob.

They all sailed up to Jericho.
They all sailed up to Jericho.
Jerry, Jerry, co, co, co.
Jerry, Jerry, co, co, co.
They all sailed up to Jericho.

They should have gone to Amsterdam.
They should have gone to Amsterdam.
Amster, Amster, sh, sh, sh.
Amster, Amster, sh, sh, sh.
Mustn't say that naughty word.

86

There Were Three Jolly Fishermen

I think I'll say it anyway.
I think I'll say it anyway.
Any, any, way, way, way.
Any, any, way, way, way.
I think I'll say it anyway.

They should have gone to Amsterdam.
They should have gone to Amsterdam.
Amster, Amster, dam, dam, dam.
Amster, Amster, dam, dam, dam.
They should have gone to Amsterdam.

The Old Family Toothbrush

To the tune of "The Old Oaken Bucket"

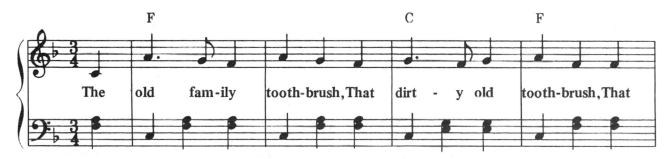

The old fam-ily tooth-brush, That dirt - y old tooth-brush, That

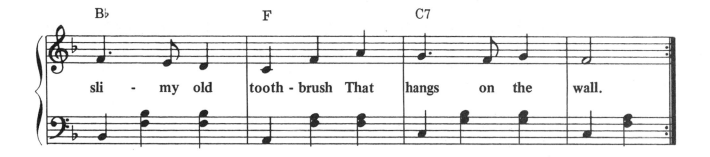

sli - my old tooth - brush That hangs on the wall.

The old family toothbrush,
That dirty old toothbrush,
That slimy old toothbrush
That hangs on the wall.

Oh, first it was Father's,
And then it was Mother's,
And next it was Sister's
And now it is mine.

Oh, Father he used it,
And Mother abused it,
And Sister refused it,
And now it is mine.

The old family toothbrush,
That dirty old toothbrush,
That slimy old toothbrush
That hangs on the wall.

There's a Hole in the Bucket

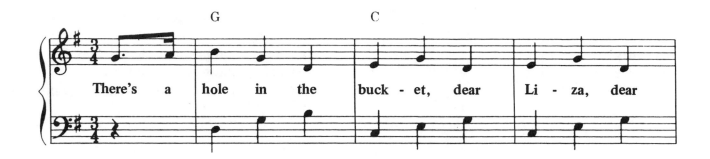

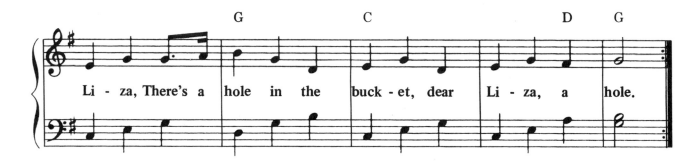

There's a hole in the bucket, dear Liza,
    dear Liza,
There's a hole in the bucket, dear Liza,
    a hole.

Then mend it, dear Henry, dear Henry,
    dear Henry,
Then mend it, dear Henry, dear Henry,
    mend it.

With what shall I mend it, dear Liza,
    dear Liza,
With what shall I mend it, dear Liza,
    with what?

With straw, dear Henry, dear Henry,
    dear Henry,
With straw, dear Henry, dear Henry,
    with straw.

The straw is too long, dear Liza, dear
    Liza,
The straw is too long, dear Liza, too
    long.

Then cut it, dear Henry, dear Henry,
    dear Henry,
Then cut it, dear Henry, dear Henry,
    cut it.

With what shall I cut it, dear Liza, dear
    Liza,
With what shall I cut it, dear Liza, with
    what?

With a knife, dear Henry, dear Henry,
    dear Henry,
With a knife, dear Henry, dear Henry,
    a knife.

The knife is too blunt, dear Liza, dear
    Liza,
The knife is too blunt, dear Liza, too
    blunt.

Then sharpen it, dear Henry, dear
    Henry, dear Henry,
Then sharpen it, dear Henry, dear
    Henry, sharpen it.

There's a Hole in the Bucket

With what shall I sharpen it, dear Liza,
    dear Liza,
With what shall I sharpen it, dear Liza,
    with what?

With a stone, dear Henry, dear Henry,
    dear Henry,
With a stone, dear Henry, dear Henry,
    a stone.

But the stone is too dry, dear Liza,
    dear Liza,
But the stone is too dry, dear Liza, too
    dry.

Then wet it, dear Henry, dear Henry,
    dear Henry,
Then wet it, dear Henry, dear Henry,
    wet it.

With what shall I wet it, dear Liza, dear
    Liza,
With what shall I wet it, dear Liza, with
    what?

With water, dear Henry, dear Henry,
    dear Henry,
With water, dear Henry, dear Henry,
    with water.

In what shall I get it, dear Liza, dear
    Liza,
In what shall I get it, dear Liza, in
    what?

In a bucket, dear Henry, dear Henry,
    dear Henry,
In a bucket, dear Henry, dear Henry, in
    a bucket.

But there's a hole in the bucket, dear
    Liza, dear Liza,
There's a hole in the bucket, dear Liza,
    a hole.

John Jacob Jingleheimer Schmidt

John Jacob Jingleheimer Schmidt—
His name is my name, too.
Whenever we go out,
The people always shout:
"There goes John Jacob Jingleheimer
    Schmidt"—
Dah, dah, dah, dah, dah, dah, dah,"

(*and repeat*).

Rise and Shine

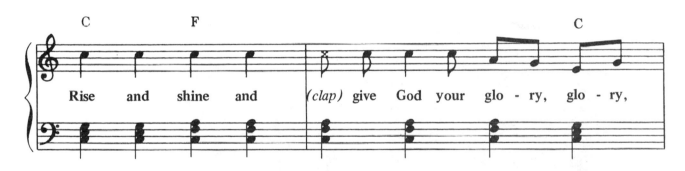

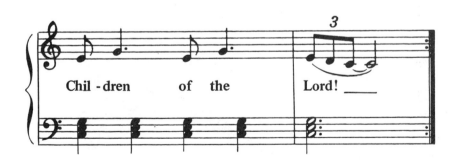

Oh, rise and shine, and give God your
    glory, glory,
Rise and shine, and give God your
    glory, glory,
Rise and shine, and (*clap*) give God
    your glory, glory,
Children of the Lord!

The Lord said to Noah, "There's gonna
    be a flood-y, flood-y,"
The Lord said to Noah, "There's gonna
    be a flood-y, flood-y.
Get your children (*clap*) out of the
    muddy, muddy"
Children of the Lord!

Rise and Shine

The Lord said to Noah, "You'd better
    build an ark-y, ark-y,"
Lord said to Noah, "You'd better build
    an ark-y, ark-y,
Build it out of (*clap*) birchy bark-y,
    bark-y,"
Children of the Lord!

The animals they came in, they came in
    by two-sy, two-sy,
Animals, they came in, they came in by
    two-sy, two-sy,
Elephants and (*clap*) kangaroo-sy,
    roo-sy,
Children of the Lord!

It rained and rained for 40 nights and 40
    daysies,
Rained and rained for 40 nights and 40
    daysies,
Drove those animals (*clap*) nearly
    crazy, crazy,
Children of the Lord!

Noah, he looked up and saw a dove-y,
    dove-y,
Noah, he looked up and saw a dove-y,
    dove-y,
Saw it up in (*clap*) heaven above-y,
    bove-y,
Children of the Lord!

Rise and Shine

The sun came out and dried up the
    land-y, land-y
Sun came out and dried up the land-y,
    land-y,
Everything was (*clap*) fine and dandy,
    dandy,
Children of the Lord!

The animals came off, came off by
    threesies, threesies,
Animals came off, came off by three-
    sies, threesies,
They'd heard about those (*clap*) birds
    and beesies, beesies,
Children of the Lord!

This is the end of, the end of my song,
    song,
This is the end of, the end of my song,
    song,
Hope it's not too (*clap*) long, long,
    long,
Children of the Lord!

This is the end of, the end of my story,
    story,
This is the end of, the end of my story,
    story,
Everything is (*clap*) hunky dory, dory,
Children of the Lord!

Rise and shine and give God your glory,
    glory,
Rise and shine and give God your glory,
    glory,
Rise and shine and (*clap*) give God your
    glory, glory,
Children of the Lord!

The Slithery D

The slithery D
Slipped into the sea.
It got all the others,
But it won't get me.

Oh, you won't get me,
You slithery D.
You got all the others,
But you won't get . . . .

INDEX OF FIRST LINES

A capital ship for an ocean trip 82
All around the cobbler's bench 58
Around the corner and under a tree 74
A sailor went to sea sea sea 65
As I was walking down the street 78
"Ba-rump," went the little green frog 14
B ay bay, B ee bee 63
Chomp, chomp, nibble, nibble, yum, yum, yum 34
Christopher McCracken went a fishing for some crabs 48
Do your ears hang low? 66
Five little monkeys walked along the shore 52
Fuzzy Wuzzy was a bear 60
Here we sit like birds in the wilderness 35
I am slowly going crazy 69
I had a rooster and the rooster pleased me 22
I know a man named Dirty Bill 39
I'm wild about horns on automobiles 67
In a cavern, in a canyon, excavating for a mine 40
I sat next to the Duchess at tea 26
I want—I want a malted 36
I wish I was a ranasasorius 62
John Jacob Jingleheimer Schmidt 90
Let's go bowling in Bowling Green 64
Little Arabella Miller found a furry caterpillar 43
Little Peter Rabbit had a fly upon his ear 19
Lulabel, where are you going? 50
Mud, mud, glorious, mud 79
No matter how young a prune may be 27
Oh, I'm bringing home a baby bumble bee 8
Oh, I'm 99 miles from home 72
Oh, I'm walkin' round the corner 76
Oh, I stuck my head in the little skunk hole 53
Oh, it's beans, beans, beans that turn us into fiends 28
Oh, rise and shine and give God your glory, glory 91
Oh, the horse went around with his foot off the ground 16
Old Joe Clarke's a fine old man 44
Old Mrs. Lazibones and her dirty daughter 46
Old Mother Leary left a lantern in the shed 38
One bottle pop, two bottle pop, three bottle pop 80
One flea fly flew up the flu 11
One little—two little—three little witches 75
On top of my pizza—all covered with sauce 31
Poor Roger is dead and gone to his grave 70
Reuben, Reuben, I've been thinking 68
She sailed away on a sunny, summer day 54
Six little ducks that I once knew 18
Susie, oh, Susie, oh, where is your goose? 15
Sweet Rosie O'Grady, she was a seamstress by birth 42
Ten more days of vacation 73
The ants go marching one by one 6
The first grasshopper jumped right over the second
    grasshopper's back 10
The old family toothbrush, that dirty old toothbrush 87
The other day I saw a bear 56
There are three ways to get peanut butter off the roof of your
    mouth 33
There once was a woman who gobbled Swiss cheese 32
There's a hole in the bucket 88
There was a Bee-eye-ee-eye-ee 12
There were three jolly fishermen 86
The slithery D slipped into the sea 94
Three green speckled frogs sat upon a speckled log 20
You take the peanut butter and you spread it 30

INDEX

Alphabet Song, 63
Amsterdam, 86
Ants Go Marching, 6
Arabella Miller, 43
Around the Corner, 74
Automobiles, 67; see Cars

Baby, 24
Baby Bumble Bee, 8
Bach, Johann Sebastian, 36
Bath, 50
Beans, 28
Bear, 60; Song, 56
Bedbugs, 77
Bees, 8, 12
Billboard Song, 78
Bill, Dirty, 39
Birds in the Wilderness, 35
Bowling Green, 64
Bread, 28, 35
Breakfast, 77
Bucket, 88
Bumble Bee, 8

Cake, 28
Cars, 24; see Automobiles
Cat, 15, 23, 45
Catch a Wiffer Woffer, 76
Caterpillar, 43
Cheese, 28
Chewing Gum, 34
Chocolate Malted, 36
Christopher McCracken, 48
Civilization, 73
Clementine, 40
Clocks, 24
Computers, 24
Cow, 24, 45; Mrs. Leary's, 38
Crabs, 48
Crocodile, 54

Dessert, 35
Dinosaur, 9
Dirty Bill, 39
Dog, 68
Do Your Ears Hang Low, 66
Duchess at Tea, 26
Ducks, 15, 18, 24

Ears, 66
Eenie, meenie and a miney moh, 76
Elephants, 92

Fire, 38
Fish, 15
Fishermen, 86
Fishing, 48
Five Little Monkeys, 52
Flea Fly Song, 11
Fly, 19
Food songs, 25–36
Frogs, 14, 15, 20
Fuzzy Wuzzy, 60

Glunk, Glunk, Glunk, 14
Goat, 15

Goose, 15
Grand Fugue, 36
Grapes, 30
Grasshopper Song, 10
Grave, 70
Guitars, 24
Gum Song, 34

Halloween, 75
Henry, 88
Hog, 15
Hole in the bucket, 88
Home, 72, 73
Horns, 24, 67
Horse Went Around, 16
House, 45

I Am Slowly Going Crazy, 69
I Had a Rooster, 22
I'm a Nut, 67
I Want a Chocolate Malted, 36
I Wish I Was, 62

Jailer, 77
Jelly, 30
Jet planes, 68
John Jacob Jingleheimer Schmidt, 90
June bug, 62

Kangaroos, 92
Knees, 32

Leap frog, 11
Leary, Mother, 38
Let's Go Bowling in Bowling Green, 64
Little Peter Rabbit, 19
Little Skunk Hole, 53
Liza, 88
Lulabel, 50

Malted, 36
Marching songs, 6, 72, 73
Meat, 28, 35
Miller, Arabella, 43
Monkeys, 52, 58, 68
Mouse, 15, 59
Mud, Mud, Glorious Mud, 79
Mule, 45
Mushrooms, 31
Musical instruments, 24

Night light, 68
99 Miles from Home, 72
Noah, 91
New York County Jail, 77

O'Grady, Sweet Rosie, 42
Old Family Toothbrush, 87
Old Joe Clarke, 44
Old Mother Leary, 38
Old Mrs. Lazibones, 46
One Bottle Pop, 80
On Top of My Pizza, 31

Peanut Butter, 33; Song, 30
Pears, 28

Peas, 28
Peter Rabbit, 19
Pickles, 77
Pie, 28
Pig, 15, 24, 59
Pizza, 31
Policeman, 77
Poor Roger is Dead, 70
Pop Goes the Weasel!, 58
Prune Song, 27

Quartermaster Corps, 28
Questions, 69

Rabbit, 19
Ranasasorius, 62
Rattlesnake, 9
Re-papa-tame-aye-ee, 62
Reuben, Reuben, 68
Rise and Shine, 91
Roaches, 77
Roger, 70
Rooster, 22
Round, 36

Sailor Went to Sea Sea Sea, 65
Sandwich, 31
Schmidt, John Jacob Jingleheimer, 90
Sergeant Major, 74
Ship, 82
Six Little Ducks, 18
Skunk, 53
Smile on the Crocodile, 54
Snake: rattle, 9; water, 15
Soup, 28, 35
Stew, 28
Supper, 45
Sweet Rosie O'Grady, 42
Swiss Cheese Song, 32

Taxi, 69
Tea, 26
There's a Hole in the Bucket, 88
There Was a Bee-Eye-Eee-Eye-Ee, 12
There Were 3 Jolly Fishermen, 86
Three Green Speckled Frogs, 20
Three Little Witches, 75
Three Ways to Get Peanut Butter Off
    the Roof of Your Mouth, 33
Tiddlywinks, 33
Toccata in G Minor, 36
Toothbrush, 87
Trains, 24
Turtle, 9, 62

Vacation, 73
Virus, 48

Walloping Windowblind, 82
Water snake, 15
Weasel, 58
We Don't Want to Go Home, 73
Where Is Your Goose?, 15
Wiffer Woffer, 76
Witches, 75